Ada Lovelace

TECHNOLOGY PIONEER

by Mary Boone

Raintree is an imprint of Capstone Global Library Limited, a company incorporated in England and Wales having its registered office at 264 Banbury Road, Oxford, OX2 7DY – Registered company number: 6695582

www.raintree.co.uk
myorders@raintree.co.uk

Text © Capstone Global Library Limited 2019
The moral rights of the proprietor have been asserted.

Edited by Erika L. Shores and Jessica Server
Designed by Charmaine Whitman
Picture research by Eric Gohl
Production by Laura Manthe
Originated by Capstone Global Library Limited
Printed and bound in India

ISBN 978 1 4747 6098 0 (hardback)   ISBN 978 1 4747 6100 0 (paperback)
22 21 20 19 18   23 22 21 20 19
10 9 8 7 6 5 4 3 2 1   10 9 8 7 6 5 4 3 2 1

British Library Cataloguing in Publication Data
A full catalogue record for this book is available from the British Library.

Acknowledgements
We would like to thank the following for permission to reproduce photographs: Alamy: Colin Underhill, 19; Getty Images: Science & Society Picture Library, 15; Library of Congress: 7; New York Public Library: 6; Newscom: akg-images, 9, Heritage Images/The Print Collector, 13, UPPA/Photoshot, cover; Shutterstock: Golden Shrimp, cover & interior (backgrounds); Wikimedia: Public Domain, 5, 11, 17, 21

Every effort has been made to contact copyright holders of material reproduced in this book. Any omissions will be rectified in subsequent printings if notice is given to the publisher.

All the internet addresses (URLs) given in this book were valid at the time of going to press. However, due to the dynamic nature of the Internet, some addresses may have changed, or sites may have changed or ceased to exist since publication. While the author and publisher regret any inconvenience this may cause readers, no responsibility for any such changes can be accepted by either the author or the publisher.

Contents

CHAPTER 1

Birth of a genius

Ada Lovelace was born more than 200 years ago. But she played a big role in the way computers are used today. Other people at the time were trying to build simple machines that could add numbers. But Ada knew with the right **programming**, these machines could do more than just maths.

programming writing instructions to make a machine or computer work in a certain way

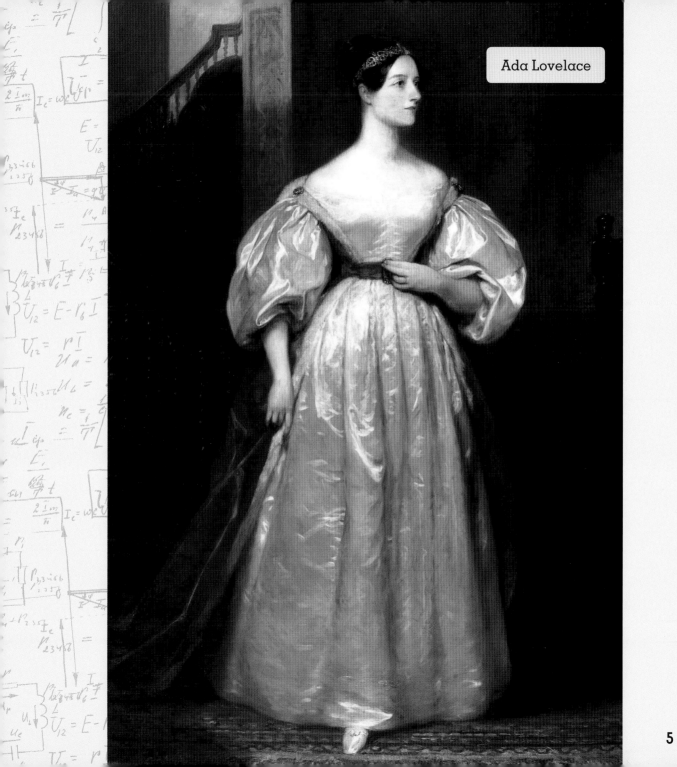

Ada Lovelace

Augusta "Ada" Byron was born in London on 10 December 1815. Her father was the famous poet Lord Byron. He left his family when Ada was a baby. She never got to know her father. He died when she was 8 years old.

Ada as a child

graduate finish studying at university

Lord Byron

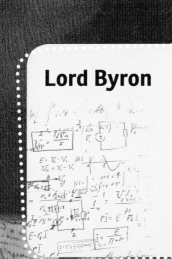

Lord Byron was known for his poems and his strange behaviour. At university, he was angry that rules stopped him from having a dog. So he got a pet bear instead! Lord Byron said there was no rule against bears. It stayed with him until he **graduated**.

Ada's mother, Anne Isabella Milbanke, was known as Lady Byron. Anne wanted her only child to get a good education. At the time, it was unusual for girls to study maths and science. But that's exactly what Ada did.

FACT As a child, Ada was often ill. When she got the measles, she had to stay in bed for a year.

Anne Isabella Milbanke

CHAPTER 2

A mind for numbers

Even as a child, it was easy to see Ada had a talent for both numbers and languages. By the age of 12, she had drawn detailed plans for a flying machine. Her design had a pair of giant wings. It was powered by a **steam engine**.

steam engine engine that gets power by heating water to make steam

"Religion to me is science,
and science is religion."

Ada Lovelace

Ada's mother employed **tutors** to teach her. One tutor was **astronomer** and **mathematician** Mary Somerville. Somerville introduced 17-year-old Ada to mathematician and inventor Charles Babbage. Ada was very interested in Babbage's plan to build what he called the "Difference Engine". He said it would be able to do difficult maths problems.

tutor teacher who gives lessons to just one pupil or a small group of pupils

astronomer scientist who studies stars, planets and other objects in space

mathematician person who studies maths

Charles Babbage

Ada visited Babbage's home to watch him use his invention. The machine was made of a stack of numbered wheels. It was powered by the turn of a handle. Ada had questions and ideas about the invention. She began to write letters to Babbage. He soon became her **mentor**.

Speaking out

Girls and women in the early 1800s were taught to keep their ideas to themselves. Ada Lovelace was clever and she knew it. She could not sit silently while men shared their ideas. Many people said Ada was rude because she spoke her mind.

mentor trusted teacher or guide

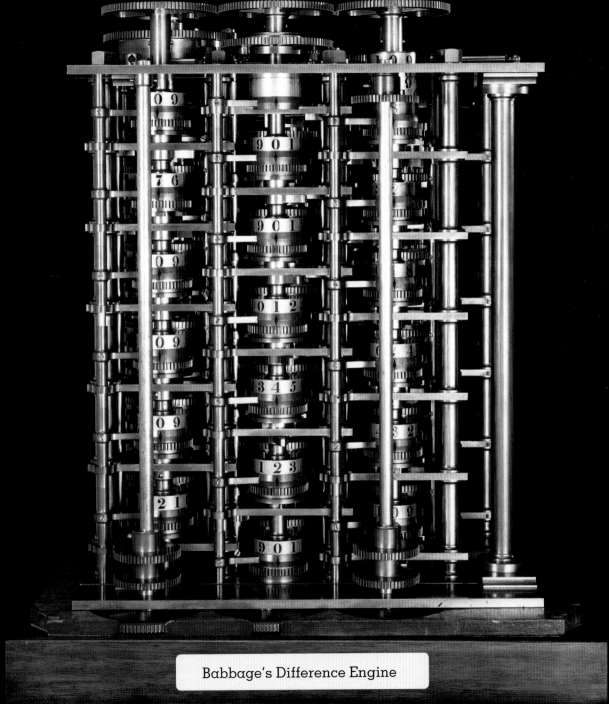

Babbage's Difference Engine

CHAPTER 3

The Lovelace legacy

In 1834 Babbage invented a more advanced mathematical machine. An article about the machine was written in French. Ada was asked to rewrite it in English. As she wrote, Ada added her own **formulas** for solving more difficult problems. She also made notes in the article. She wrote about ways in which formulas could be used as instructions to control the machine.

formula rule in science or maths that is written using numbers and symbols

Diagram for the computation by the Engine of the Numbers of Bernoulli. See Note G. (page 722 *et seq.*)

a diagram from the article on Babbage's machine

FACT In Ada's notes, she also wrote about how machines might one day understand science and even create music.

Sadly, on 27 November 1852, Ada died from cancer at the age of 36. Nearly 100 years after her death, people who studied her work discovered how brilliant it was. People began to call her "the world's first computer programmer".

FACT Ada Lovelace Day is held every year on the second Tuesday of October. It celebrates women working in science, technology, engineering and maths.

Ada Augusta Lovelace memorial in Leicestershire, England

Ada was a **pioneer** in computer programming. Her important work has been noted in books and films. In 1980 the US Department of Defense named its new computer language "Ada" after her. Ada Lovelace used maths to make a difference in the world.

Family life

In 1835 Ada married William King. William was given a royal title in 1838. The couple became known as the Earl and Countess of Lovelace. Ada and William's three children were Anne, Ralph and Byron.

pioneer person who is the first to try new things

Ada in 1852

Glossary

astronomer scientist who studies stars, planets and other objects in space

formula rule in science or maths that is written using numbers and symbols

graduate finish studying at university

mathematician person who studies maths

mentor trusted teacher or guide

pioneer person who is the first to try new things

programming writing instructions to make a machine or computer work in a certain way

steam engine engine that gets power by heating water to make steam

tutor teacher who gives lessons to just one pupil or a small group of pupils

Find out more

Books

Ada Lovelace, Poet of Science: The First Computer Programmer, Diane Stanley (Simon & Schuster, 2016)

Understanding Programming and Logic (Understanding Computing), Matthew Anniss (Raintree, 2016)

Websites

www.bbc.co.uk/guides/zykx6sg
  What is code? Find out more!

www.dkfindout.com/uk/science/famous-scientists/ada-lovelace/
  Find out more about Ada Lovelace.

Comprehension questions

1. When Ada Lovelace was a child, most girls received little education. How different would the world be if girls today could not go to school?

2. Imagine you met Ada Lovelace at a party in 1843, and she told you about her ideas for a machine that could think. How would you have reacted?

Index